@CANNYCRYSTALS   CANNYCRYSTALSACADEMY.CO.UK

Hello!

My name is Mart, and I'm the Owner and Director of Canny Crystals - welcome to this 21 day Manifesting Money challenge! I'm so happy that you've chosen to join and that you're actually dedicated to enhancing your wealth and prosperity.

I wanted to do this challenge because I've been in the position and mindset of lack and scarcity; I've struggled to get through the day due to lack of finances, and I know first hand how it can have a detrimental effect on your well-being.

So what better way than to show you all these tools and techniques than to run a 21-day challenge incorporating a daily challenge to enhance your wealth, abundance and prosperity.

At the end of this challenge, hopefully you've have learned enough to feel confident about your future money mindset.

And what's more is that once you've got this booklet, you can do this challenge again at any point in your life! There really are no rules here, and the best thing is that each time you do it, you'll uncover more and more about your limiting beliefs.

If you want to go further after completing the 21 days, I offer a Manifesting Money Masterclass 6 week course on the Academy, which you can gain lifetime access to by visiting cannycrystalsacademy.co.uk and selecting the course.

Apart from that, let's get started on this 21-day challenge!

@CANNYCRYSTALS   CANNYCRYSTALSACADEMY.CO.UK

Day 1 — TRACKING YOUR MONEY

Let's start from the top!

The number one way to help you manifest more wealth into your life is to first get familiar with what you currently have. How else would we be able to measure any form of improvement? Tracking your money is an essential practice for achieving financial growth and manifesting abundance. By understanding your current financial situation, you can identify areas of improvement and make conscious choices moving forward.

Becoming aware of your income and any money entering into your life is the first step towards creating positive changes in your financial life. So for the first exercise, I want you to use the tracker on the following pages to write down every bit of money or things you're gifted, every single day for the next 3 weeks!

I want to encourage you to approach today's exercise with curiosity and a non-judgmental mindset. Try to be as thorough and accurate in your tracking as you can, ensuring you include all sources of income, no matter how small! If you find a penny on the street, add it on to the tracker! You're bought a coffee by a colleague, put it on your tracker.

Not only will this make you realise how much money actually comes your way, but it'll also help you realise that you can actively manifest as much as you want in your life. We're not interested in expenses for this exercise, just income!

Remember, manifesting wealth is a journey that requires consistent effort and a positive mindset. By taking small, daily steps towards your financial goals, you'll be on your way to living the life you desire.

Day 1 — TRACKING YOUR MONEY

Exercise: Track all the money that has come to you at the end of each day of this challenge. Whether it be your paid wage, money that a family member or friend gave you, a tax rebate you got, whatever it is, pop it in the money column. Do the same with freebies you receive such as gifts from friends, coffees from colleagues, etc. and pop these in the value column. It WILL surprise you when you see on paper how much money crosses your account each month!

DATE	MONEY	VALUE	TOTALS

@CANNYCRYSTALS   CANNYCRYSTALSACADEMY.CO.UK

Day 1 TRACKING YOUR MONEY

DATE	MONEY	VALUE	TOTALS

TOTALS

@CANNYCRYSTALS   CANNYCRYSTALSACADEMY.CO.UK

Day 1 — TRACKING YOUR MONEY

Once you've filled in every single day, add up each column in the bottom "totals" line.

What do you notice about these totals?

- Are they more than you thought that they would be?

- Have you received more in value of free gifts and items than you have money?

- Are there any surprises that have come to you since doing this exercise daily?

Each day, as well as an exercise to complete, you'll also see on the next page that there will be space for you to write three things that you're grateful for.

By expressing gratitude, we open ourselves up to all the other opportunities of goodness that can head our way. Some people like to start their mornings with this to set them up for the day ahead, and some prefer to do this last thing at night to journal out and release the energy of their day before bed.

Please do whichever works best for you; there are no right or wrong ways about this.

You'll also see a daily affirmation to repeat throughout each day. Repeat this whenever you remember to, and for best results, do it whilst looking at yourself in the mirror. When we repeat affirmations, we are essentially creating new, positive neural pathways in our brains that will eventually become just as strong – if not stronger – than our negative ones. Head to the next page to check out day 1's affirmation.

Day 1 — TRACKING YOUR MONEY

Tasks for the day

1. TRACK ALL INCOME ON LOG

2. LIST 3 THINGS THAT YOU'RE GRATEFUL FOR TODAY

3. REPEAT YOUR DAILY AFFIRMATION AT LEAST 3 TIMES THROUGHOUT THE DAY

SHARE YOUR WINS ON SOCIAL MEDIA - TAG @CANNYCRYSTALS

@CANNYCRYSTALS    CANNYCRYSTALSACADEMY.CO.UK

Day 1 — TRACKING YOUR MONEY

Gratitude

I am so grateful for....

because...

Affirmation of the day

"I AM A MONEY MAGNET - MONEY FLOWS TO ME EFFORTLESSLY"

@CANNYCRYSTALS   CANNYCRYSTALSACADEMY.CO.UK

Day 2 — EFT / TAPPING

EFT stands for Emotional Freedom Techniques. It's a therapeutic technique that combines elements of acupressure and psychology to address emotional and physical issues.

While EFT is not a direct tool for manifesting money, it can help shift your mindset and remove any emotional barriers that might be blocking your ability to attract financial abundance. When it comes to manifesting money, our beliefs, attitudes, and mindset play a crucial role. If you have negative beliefs or limiting thoughts around money, such as feelings of unworthiness or scarcity, it can create energetic blocks that impede the flow of abundance into your life.

EFT can be used as a tool to address these negative beliefs and transform them into positive ones. By tapping on specific acupressure points while focusing on the negative beliefs or emotions associated with money, you can release and clear those energetic blocks. This process helps to shift your mindset and create space for more positive and abundant thoughts and beliefs.

EFT can be a powerful tool to address deep-seated beliefs and emotions around money. By releasing negative energy and shifting your mindset towards abundance, you can create a more favorable environment for manifesting money.

It's important to note that while EFT can be beneficial, it is just one aspect of the manifestation process, and taking action and aligning your thoughts, feelings, and behaviors with your financial goals is also essential.

With all that said, let's have a crack at Day 2's exercise, tapping for raising your wealth and abundance!

Day 2 — EFT / TAPPING

Exercise: Follow the tapping instructions below to release blocks.

Setup Statement (Repeat 3 times whilst tapping on the karate-chop point on the side of your hand):

"Even though I have this belief that money is hard to come by, I deeply and completely accept myself and choose to release this belief now"

"Even though I feel scarcity around money, I deeply and completely accept myself and open myself to a mindset of abundance and prosperity"

"Even though I've been holding onto these limiting beliefs about money, I choose to let them go and embrace a new positive perspective"

Tapping Sequence (Tap on each point 5-10 times while repeating the reminder phrase):

Eyebrow: This belief that money is hard to come by.
Side of the Eye: I've been feeling scarcity around money.
Under the Eye: These limiting beliefs I've held onto.
Under the Nose: I choose to release them now.
Chin: I am ready to let go of scarcity.
Collarbone: I release any blocks to abundance.
Under the Arm: Releasing these old beliefs about money.
Top of the Head: Embracing a mindset of abundance and prosperity.

Continue with the following two rounds on the next page, going back to the eyebrow point and working your way round 2 more cycles...

Day 2 — EFT / TAPPING

Eyebrow: Releasing this belief that money is hard to come by.
Side of the Eye: I let go of scarcity and embrace abundance.
Under the Eye: I release any fear or anxiety around money.
Under the Nose: I choose to shift my mindset and attract prosperity.
Chin: I release all the limitations I've placed on myself.
Collarbone: I open myself up to new opportunities for abundance.
Under the Arm: I release these old patterns and welcome positive change.
Top of the Head: I embrace a mindset of abundance and prosperity.

Eyebrow: I allow money to flow effortlessly into my life.
Side of the Eye: I release resistance to receiving financial abundance.
Under the Eye: I am worthy of experiencing wealth.
Under the Nose: I let go of any beliefs that limit my success.
Chin: I choose to align my thoughts and actions with abundance.
Collarbone: I welcome a positive relationship with money.
Under the Arm: I am open to receiving and manifesting money with ease.
Top of the Head: I embrace a mindset of unlimited financial possibilities.

Take a deep breath, shake out your hands and arms, and check in with yourself. Reassess the intensity of the belief or emotion on a scale of 0 to 10. If the intensity is still high, you can repeat the tapping sequence, adjusting the statements to address any specific aspects that come up.

Remember to focus on your own personal beliefs and emotions around money and modify the script accordingly.

Day 2 — EFT / TAPPING

Tasks for the day

1. TRACK ALL INCOME ON LOG

2. TRY THE EFT/TAPPING SCRIPT AT SOME POINT TODAY

3. LIST 3 THINGS THAT YOU'RE GRATEFUL FOR TODAY

4. REPEAT YOUR DAILY AFFIRMATION AT LEAST 3 TIMES

SHARE YOUR WINS ON SOCIAL MEDIA - TAG @CANNYCRYSTALS

@CANNYCRYSTALS   CANNYCRYSTALSACADEMY.CO.UK

Day 2

EFT / TAPPING

Gratitude

I am so grateful for....

because...

Affirmation of the day

"I AM DESERVING OF WEALTH AND FINANCIAL ABUNDANCE"

@CANNYCRYSTALS   CANNYCRYSTALSACADEMY.CO.UK

Day 3: SUBLIMINAL AFFIRMATIONS

Subliminal affirmations are positive statements that are presented to the subconscious mind at a level below conscious awareness. They're often used as a tool for self-improvement and personal development.

The idea behind subliminal affirmations is that by bypassing the conscious mind, the subconscious can more readily accept and internalise positive suggestions, leading to desired changes in beliefs, attitudes, and behaviours.

As powerful as affirmations are, our conscious mind and our rational thoughts sometimes reject the statements as not being true. For example, if I said to myself in the mirror "I am so wealthy, money comes to me easily", my conscious mind might be saying to me "no you're not - you have to work hard for the money!" - which is the opposite of what we're trying to achieve. The path of least resistance is to bypass this conscious voice!

When it comes to attracting financial abundance, subliminal affirmations can be used to reprogram your subconscious mind to adopt beliefs and attitudes that support abundance and prosperity. Repetition and consistency are key when it comes to subliminal affirmations. Listen to your subliminal affirmations daily, ideally multiple times a day, to reinforce the positive suggestions in your subconscious mind. Consistency and repetition are key for effective reprogramming within the brain.

You may also find it beneficial to engage with affirmations in a relaxed state. Find a quiet and comfortable space to listen to your affirmations. Relaxation techniques such as deep breathing or meditation can help you enter a receptive state for affirmations to be more impactful.

Day 3 — SUBLIMINAL AFFIRMATIONS

The most common thing people tell me when I advise them to listen to subliminal affirmations is that they "don't have time" to add yet another spiritual practice into their already hectic lives. Guess what, you don't need any more time than you already have!

Subliminals don't require any focus. You can therefore pop on some headphones and get on with your day whilst being fed with the good stuff as you crack through your daily chores and tasks.

I listen to my subliminal affirmations as I get ready for work on a morning, whilst working out, whilst taking my dog for a walk, whilst driving to meetings, whilst cooking meals, and always end my day by playing them overnight as I drift off to sleep. Your subconscious mind is ALWAYS listening.

Be patient and persistent. Subliminal affirmations work gradually, and results may take time to manifest. Be patient in your practice, trusting that your subconscious mind is absorbing the positive suggestions and working towards attracting financial abundance.

Remember that while subliminal affirmations can be a powerful tool for personal growth in many ways, they are not a substitute for action.

Take practical steps towards your financial goals alongside using affirmations, such as taking appropriate inspired actions to create multiple opportunities for abundance in your life.

Get your Subliminal Affirmations at 50% OFF by using code '21DAYS' at cannycrystals.co.uk and typing "subliminals" in the search box.

Day 3 — SUBLIMINAL AFFIRMATIONS

Tasks for the day

1. TRACK ALL INCOME ON LOG

2. TRY AND INCORPORATE LISTENING TO SUBLIMINALS TODAY

3. LIST 3 THINGS THAT YOU'RE GRATEFUL FOR TODAY

4. REPEAT YOUR DAILY AFFIRMATION AT LEAST 3 TIMES

SHARE YOUR WINS ON SOCIAL MEDIA - TAG @CANNYCRYSTALS

@CANNYCRYSTALS   CANNYCRYSTALSACADEMY.CO.UK

Day 3

SUBLIMINAL AFFIRMATIONS

Gratitude

I am so grateful for....

because...

Affirmation of the day

"I AM OPEN TO RECEIVING UNLIMITED FINANCIAL PROSPERITY"

@CANNYCRYSTALS   CANNYCRYSTALSACADEMY.CO.UK

Day 4 — TOKEN ITEMS

Token items, when used intentionally, can serve as powerful reminders and symbols that help us stay focused on our financial goals and manifest abundance.

Whether it be a crystal such as Pyrite, Moldavite, Jade, Citrine or green Aventurine (all well known for attracting prosperity) or even just something that means wealth to you, token items can play a fundamental part in achieving abundance in your life.

Here's how token items can help:

- Visual Representation: Token items, such as small objects or talismans, can visually represent your financial goals and desires. For example, you might choose a coin to symbolise wealth or a keyring representing financial freedom. When you see these items, they act as reminders of your aspirations and can strengthen your belief in achieving them.

- Anchoring Positive Emotions: Token items can evoke positive emotions associated with financial success and abundance. By holding or looking at these items, you can generate feelings of gratitude, confidence, and motivation. These emotions play a vital role in manifesting your goals by aligning your energy and mindset with abundance.

- Focus and Intention: Token items serve as focal points for your thoughts and intentions. By intentionally connecting the item with your financial goals, you reinforce your commitment and dedication to achieving them. Whenever you interact with or come across the token item, it helps bring your attention back to your financial aspirations.

Day 4 — TOKEN ITEMS

- **Affirmation and Empowerment:** Token items can be infused with affirmations or empowering messages related to your financial goals. For example, you might attach a note to the item with a statement like, "I'm a magnet for abundance" or "I attract wealth effortlessly." These affirmations, combined with the physical presence of the token item, reinforce positive beliefs and support your manifestation journey.

- **Rituals and Daily Practices:** Incorporating token items into daily rituals or practices can deepen their impact. For instance, you might hold the item during visualization or meditation sessions focused on financial abundance. You can also place the token item on your desk, in your car or in any prominent location where you can see it regularly, reminding yourself of your financial intentions and the steps you're taking to manifest them.

Remember, the power of token items lies in the intention and meaning you assign to them. Choose an item that resonates with you and your financial goals. Infuse it with positive energy, affirmations, and symbolism that align with your vision of abundance. Regularly interact with the token item and use it as a tool to reinforce your mindset, beliefs, and actions toward achieving your financial aspirations.

Today's action is therefore to have a think about what you can use as your daily token item, to bring you focus and attention back to feeling wealthy, abundant and prosperous in all areas of your life.

Use this token as a reminder that you ARE worthy of receiving money, and that it can come to you in all forms across various opportunities.

Day 4 — TOKEN ITEMS

Tasks for the day

1. TRACK ALL INCOME ON LOG

2. FIND A TOKEN ITEM TO ANCHOR YOUR THOUGHTS TO WEALTH

3. LIST 3 THINGS THAT YOU'RE GRATEFUL FOR TODAY

4. REPEAT YOUR DAILY AFFIRMATION AT LEAST 3 TIMES

SHARE YOUR WINS ON SOCIAL MEDIA - TAG @CANNYCRYSTALS

@CANNYCRYSTALS   CANNYCRYSTALSACADEMY.CO.UK

Day 4

TOKEN ITEMS

Gratitude

I am so grateful for....

because...

Affirmation of the day

"MY INCOME IS CONSTANTLY INCREASING - I AM FINANCIALLY SECURE"

@CANNYCRYSTALS    CANNYCRYSTALSACADEMY.CO.UK

Day 5 — DECLUTTERING

Decluttering can have a profound impact on our mindset, helping us align with our financial goals and manifest abundance.

Decluttering physical spaces, such as your home or workspace, creates literal space for abundance to flow into your life. By removing excess clutter and organising your surroundings, you open up room for new opportunities, ideas, and prosperity to enter. Clutter can often carry emotional weight and can be a reflection of underlying beliefs and attachments. When you declutter, you release emotional attachments to material possessions and make room for new experiences. This process helps you let go of a scarcity mindset, fear, and limitations around money, enabling a shift towards abundance.

Decluttering also allows you to reassess your values and priorities. By evaluating your possessions and deciding what truly brings you joy and adds value to your life, you align your choices with what matters most. This reflection extends beyond physical items and can guide your financial decisions, focusing resources on what truly supports your goals and aspirations. Through decluttering, you become more aware of your consumption habits. This awareness helps you make conscious choices about what you bring into your life. By adopting a more mindful approach to spending, you can redirect financial resources towards investments, experiences, and opportunities that align with your financial goals.

Decluttering can help shift your mindset from scarcity to abundance. As you let go of possessions that no longer serve you, you reinforce the belief that there is always enough and that you are deserving of abundance. This shift in mindset opens you up to new possibilities and

Day 5 — DECLUTTERING

allows you to approach financial goals with a more expansive and positive mindset.

And lastly, decluttering promotes gratitude for what you have and contentment with less. By appreciating the possessions and resources you choose to keep, you cultivate a sense of abundance and satisfaction. This mindset of gratitude attracts more abundance and reinforces the belief that you have everything you need to achieve your financial goals.

Just remember, decluttering is not just about physical possessions. It extends to decluttering your mindset, habits, and financial practices. Embrace decluttering as a holistic practice that supports your journey towards financial abundance by creating space, releasing attachments, and aligning your actions with your goals and values.

So today's action is to declutter an area of your life, and this might be something that you want to continue doing over the remainder of this 21 day challenge if you enjoy it.

Choose one area of your life; that could be a cupboard under the stairs, your purse, your car, or even your sock drawer... and I want you to go through it, and get rid of everything that no longer serves you. Thank it for serving it's purpose and let it go.

It might be a sock with a hole in, it might be random receipts in your purse that you no longer need, it could even be numerous carrier bags in your car, or lots of unopened e-mails on your phone... whatever it is, assess with yourself and ask, do I really need to keep this? Or can I let it go and create room for abundance in my life?

Day 5 — DECLUTTERING

Tasks for the day

1. TRACK ALL INCOME ON LOG

2. FIND AN AREA OF YOUR LIFE TO DECLUTTER TODAY

3. LIST 3 THINGS THAT YOU'RE GRATEFUL FOR TODAY

4. REPEAT YOUR DAILY AFFIRMATION AT LEAST 3 TIMES

SHARE YOUR WINS ON SOCIAL MEDIA - TAG @CANNYCRYSTALS

@CANNYCRYSTALS   CANNYCRYSTALSACADEMY.CO.UK

Day 5 — DECLUTTERING

Gratitude

I am so grateful for....

because...

Affirmation of the day

"I AM A POWERFUL CREATOR OF WEALTH"

@CANNYCRYSTALS   CANNYCRYSTALSACADEMY.CO.UK

Day 6 — UP-LEVEL YOUR LIFE

Improving your wealth and abundance, and upgrading your life incrementally requires a combination of planning, discipline, and consistent effort.

By making small and consistent changes, you can incrementally move yourself up the ladder of abundance!

Think of all the different areas of your life where you can make a small change. It could be:

- upgrading your crockery in your kitchen
- upgrading your shampoo or toothpaste
- upgrading your underwear or socks
- upgrading your purse or wallet
- upgrading your perfume/aftershave
- upgrading your wardrobe

Whatever area you choose to concentrate on, start small! That's the key here. If we went all out and purchased all of the above and MORE, we would probably end up resenting spending so much, whereas when we do it incrementally, we can catapult ourselves into that wealthy and prosperous life that we desire so much.

Today, choose one area of your life that you feel "poor" in. Take a look at all of the options available to you and all the different things that you could upgrade in that specific area. For example, if you choose your wardrobe as a starting point, maybe declutter some t-shirts that no longer fit you, and each month, buy yourself a couple of new ones. This way you'll slowly introduce yourself to the lifestyle that you wish to have and it won't feel like too much pressure.

Day 6

UP-LEVEL YOUR LIFE

Tasks for the day

1. TRACK ALL INCOME ON LOG

2. CHOOSE AN AREA OF YOUR LIFE TO BEGIN UPGRADING

3. LIST 3 THINGS THAT YOU'RE GRATEFUL FOR TODAY

4. REPEAT YOUR DAILY AFFIRMATION AT LEAST 3 TIMES

SHARE YOUR WINS ON SOCIAL MEDIA - TAG @CANNYCRYSTALS

@CANNYCRYSTALS   CANNYCRYSTALSACADEMY.CO.UK

Day 6 — UP-LEVEL YOUR LIFE

Gratitude

I am so grateful for....

because...

Affirmation of the day

"MONEY FLOWS INTO MY LIFE FROM MULTIPLE SOURCES"

@CANNYCRYSTALS   CANNYCRYSTALSACADEMY.CO.UK

Day 7 — VISION BOARDS

Creating a vision board can provide several benefits when it comes to wealth and financial goals. A vision board helps you clarify your financial aspirations and brings focus to your goals. By visually representing your desires, you gain a clear picture of what you want to achieve financially, making it easier to stay motivated and aligned with your objectives.

Visualisation is a powerful tool for manifesting your desires. When you regularly see images of your financial goals on your vision board, you are more likely to visualise and believe in your ability to achieve them. This visualisation process helps attract the opportunities, resources, and mindset needed to manifest wealth.

Your vision board acts as a source of inspiration and motivation. Seeing your goals and dreams visually displayed can reignite your passion, reminding you of the reasons why you are pursuing financial success. During challenging times, your vision board can provide a boost of motivation to keep moving forward.

Your vision board aligns your conscious and subconscious mind. As you consistently expose yourself to the images and affirmations on your board, your subconscious mind starts accepting them as truth. This alignment helps shift your beliefs, thoughts, and behaviours towards attracting wealth and opportunities.

By creating a vision board centred around wealth, you shift your mindset from scarcity to abundance. The visual representation of abundance on your board serves as a constant reminder that wealth and prosperity are within your reach. It helps you cultivate a positive mindset and attract more abundance into your life.

Day 7 — VISION BOARDS

Your vision board allows you to track your progress and celebrate achievements along the way. As you accomplish financial milestones, you can add new images or adjust existing ones on your board to reflect your evolving goals. This process helps you stay engaged and motivated throughout your wealth-building journey.

The law of attraction suggests that like attracts like. By focusing your attention and energy on your financial goals through your vision board, you align yourself with the energy of wealth and abundance. This alignment can attract opportunities, resources, and people that support your financial growth.

You don't have to create a vision board like it's the 1990's! There's no longer a need for scissors, old magazines and a Pritt Stick (if you know what one of those are, you're showing your age!) - you can now make your own vision board on something as simple as an app on your phone! Or you could even just create it on a programme such as Canva, or PhotoShop!

However you choose to do it, make sure that it's personal to you and that all the images that you use inspire you internally to light that fire and raise your abundance! Have a go - it's a lot more fun than you probably think!

Once you've created your vision board, put it in a prominant place that you're going to see it on a daily basis; this may be on your phone lock screen, your desktop or laptop home screen, or even printed and put on your bedroom or office wall. Make sure that each time you see it, you think of how amazing you'll feel once you have these items!

Day 7 — VISION BOARDS

Tasks for the day

1. TRACK ALL INCOME ON LOG

2. CREATE YOUR PERFECT VISION BOARD

3. LIST 3 THINGS THAT YOU'RE GRATEFUL FOR TODAY

4. REPEAT YOUR DAILY AFFIRMATION AT LEAST 3 TIMES

SHARE YOUR WINS ON SOCIAL MEDIA - TAG @CANNYCRYSTALS

@CANNYCRYSTALS   CANNYCRYSTALSACADEMY.CO.UK

Day 7 — VISION BOARDS

Gratitude

I am so grateful for....

because...

Affirmation of the day

"WEALTH AND ABUNDANCE ARE MY NATURAL STATE OF BEING"

@CANNYCRYSTALS    CANNYCRYSTALSACADEMY.CO.UK

Day 8 — MEDITATE AND VISUALISE

Meditation and visualisation are powerful practices that can greatly contribute to your spiritual growth and enhance your overall sense of well-being, including your wealth and abundance. While they are not a magic formula for instant material success, they can positively influence your mindset, mindset, and inner state, which in turn can attract opportunities and foster a prosperous mindset.

Meditation is a practice that involves training your mind to focus and redirect your thoughts. By regularly engaging in meditation, you can cultivate a greater sense of mindfulness and self-awareness. This heightened state of awareness allows you to recognise and release any limiting beliefs or negative thought patterns that may be hindering your financial abundance. It provides an opportunity to quiet the incessant chatter of the mind and create space for clarity and inspiration to arise. It can help you connect with your inner wisdom and intuition, allowing you to make more informed and aligned decisions regarding your financial goals. Moreover, meditation reduces stress and anxiety, which are often roadblocks to attracting abundance. By cultivating a calm and centred mind through meditation, you create an environment conducive to attracting and manifesting prosperity.

Visualisation, on the other hand, involves using your imagination to create vivid mental images of your desired outcomes. By visualising yourself already in possession of the wealth and abundance you seek, you engage the power of your subconscious mind to manifest those desires into reality. When you consistently and vividly imagine yourself living a prosperous life, you begin to align your thoughts, emotions, and actions with that vision. This alignment sets in motion a series of events and synchronicities that bring you closer to your goals.

Day 8 — MEDITATE AND VISUALISE

Visualisation is not just about wishful thinking; it is about creating a detailed and sensory-rich experience in your mind. By incorporating all your senses and emotions into your visualisations, you make them more tangible and believable. As you consistently practice visualisation, you start to reprogram your subconscious mind, which is a powerful tool for shaping your reality. Your subconscious mind cannot distinguish between what is real and what is imagined, so by repeatedly visualising your desired wealth and abundance, you start to attract circumstances and opportunities that align with that vision.

When meditation and visualisation are combined, their effects can be even more profound. Meditation clears the mind and creates a receptive state, while visualisation provides a focused direction for your intentions. By meditating before engaging in visualisation, you can quiet the mind and access deeper levels of awareness, making your visualisations more potent and effective.

Today, try and find just 5-10 minutes to quieten your mind somewhere that you won't be disturbed. Once you've managed to do this, visualise your end goal. Bring to the forefront any associated emotions such as happiness, joy, fulfilment, excitedness, love, gratitude or optimism. Connect with those emotions as you continue to imagine yourself in that dream life of abundance and wealth.

The more you do this, the easier it will get. Visualising yourself in that end goal will help your mind to decipher how it's going to get there and put things into motion to allow you to achieve all that you want, and more. You can even hold a crystal of choice whilst visualising for an added boost! Check out the "wealth and prosperity" section of cannycrystals.co.uk for inspiration!

Day 8 — MEDITATE AND VISUALISE

Tasks for the day

1. TRACK ALL INCOME ON LOG

2. INCORPORATE 5-10 MINUTES OF VISUALISING YOUR DREAM GOAL

3. LIST 3 THINGS THAT YOU'RE GRATEFUL FOR TODAY

4. REPEAT YOUR DAILY AFFIRMATION AT LEAST 3 TIMES

SHARE YOUR WINS ON SOCIAL MEDIA - TAG @CANNYCRYSTALS

@CANNYCRYSTALS   CANNYCRYSTALSACADEMY.CO.UK

Day 8 — MEDITATE AND VISUALISE

Gratitude

I am so grateful for....

because...

Affirmation of the day

"WEALTH COMES TO ME NATURALLY"

@CANNYCRYSTALS   CANNYCRYSTALSACADEMY.CO.UK

Day 9 — ABUNDANCE BOWL

An abundance bowl is a concept rooted in the principles of abundance and manifestation. It's a symbolic representation of attracting and embodying prosperity, wealth, and abundance into our life. The abundance bowl is often used as a tool for focusing intentions, raising vibrations, and inviting positive energy into various aspects of life, including financial well-being.

The abundance bowl typically consists of a decorative bowl or container filled with a combination of specific elements that are believed to enhance abundance and prosperity. These elements can vary depending on personal beliefs, cultural practices, and individual preferences. However, common items often found in abundance bowls include:

Crystals: Many people believe that certain crystals and gemstones possess an energy that can attract abundance and wealth. Examples of stones associated with abundance include citrine, pyrite, green aventurine, jade, malachite and moldavite.

Currency: Placing actual currency or symbolic representations of money, such as fake bills or coins, in the abundance bowl can symbolise a desire for financial prosperity and abundance.

Symbols of abundance: Adding symbols such as a wealth deity, lucky charms, or representations of abundance, like golden figurines or symbols from various cultures, can serve as visual reminders and focus points for attracting prosperity.

Affirmations and intentions: Writing affirmations or intentions related to wealth and abundance on small pieces of paper and placing them in the abundance bowl can reinforce positive beliefs and invite the manifestation of desired outcomes.

Day 9 — ABUNDANCE BOWL

The importance of assisting yourself with raising wealth and abundance in life lies in the potential to cultivate a positive mindset and create favourable conditions for financial success. Here are a few reasons why this focus can be significant:

Shift in mindset: By actively engaging in practices such as creating an abundance bowl, you direct your attention towards abundance, shifting your mindset from scarcity to abundance. This change in perspective can open up new possibilities, increase motivation, and attract opportunities that align with your desires.

Law of Attraction: The law of attraction suggests that like attracts like, meaning that your thoughts and emotions play a crucial role in manifesting your reality. By intentionally focusing on wealth and abundance, you are more likely to attract circumstances, people, and resources that support your financial goals.

Increased gratitude and appreciation: Practices related to abundance often encourage gratitude and appreciation for what you already have. Gratitude fosters a positive outlook, enhances satisfaction with your current situation, and opens the doors for even more blessings to flow into your life.

Empowerment and action: Raising wealth and abundance isn't solely about wishful thinking; it also involves taking action and making empowered decisions. By actively engaging in practices and rituals that promote abundance, you cultivate a sense of agency and responsibility for your financial well-being.

Today, get yourself a decorative bowl and fill it with as many things mentioned as possible and place it in the wealth corner of your home (Google "Feng Shui Bagua" to find yours).

Day 9 — ABUNDANCE BOWL

Tasks for the day

1. TRACK ALL INCOME ON LOG

2. CREATE AND PLACE YOUR ABUNDANCE BOWL

3. LIST 3 THINGS THAT YOU'RE GRATEFUL FOR TODAY

4. REPEAT YOUR DAILY AFFIRMATION AT LEAST 3 TIMES

SHARE YOUR WINS ON SOCIAL MEDIA - TAG @CANNYCRYSTALS

@CANNYCRYSTALS   CANNYCRYSTALSACADEMY.CO.UK

Day 9 — ABUNDANCE BOWL

Gratitude

I am so grateful for....

because...

Affirmation of the day

"I AM IN FULL ALIGNMENT WITH THE ENERGY OF ABUNDANCE"

@CANNYCRYSTALS — CANNYCRYSTALSACADEMY.CO.UK

Day 10 — TALK ABOUT MONEY

Remember when you were younger, and someone would give you a birthday cake with candles and tell you, "blow out the candles and make a wish, but don't tell anyone or it won't come true"? I'm here to tell you the opposite! While some may view this as merely wishful thinking or a superstitious belief, there are psychological and practical reasons why it can be beneficial to talk about what you want to achieve in life.

When you talk about what you want, whether it's related to money or any other aspect of life, you're forced to articulate and clarify your desires. This process helps you gain a deeper understanding of what you truly want and allows you to set clear goals. By vocalising your aspirations, you bring them to the forefront of your mind, making it easier to create a plan of action to achieve them.

By openly discussing your financial goals, you increase your focus and motivation. Sharing your intentions with others creates a sense of accountability, as people around you become aware of your desires. This added sense of responsibility can motivate you to take consistent action towards your goals, knowing that others are aware of your aspirations.

When you talk about what you want, you open up the possibility of finding support and assistance from others. You never know who in your network might have valuable connections, resources, or advice to help you on your financial journey.

By vocalising your intentions, you create opportunities for others to offer support, guidance, or even collaborate with you towards your goals.

Day 10 — TALK ABOUT MONEY

The subconscious mind plays a significant role in manifesting our desires. By regularly talking about what you want, you embed these thoughts and intentions into your subconscious. This repetitive reinforcement helps to shift your mindset, making you more open and receptive to opportunities and ideas that align with your financial goals. Just like with affirmations, you're speaking your desires into existence!

The law of attraction, a popular concept in manifestation, suggests that positive or negative thoughts and emotions can attract corresponding experiences into our lives. By consistently discussing your financial goals and visualising the abundance you desire, you send out positive energy and attract circumstances and opportunities that align with your intentions.

However, it's important to note that talking about what you want is not a substitute for action. It's crucial to combine your intentions with focused effort, learning, and strategic planning to achieve financial success.

Manifestation is not about passively waiting for money to magically appear but about aligning your thoughts, emotions, and actions to create the circumstances and opportunities necessary for financial abundance.

This is where so many people go wrong when trying to manifest money into their lives. They'll speak it out of their minds into the Universe and put their intentions out there, but then won't do anything to take action. So today, I want you to tell 3 people that you speak to throughout the day, and tell them where you want to be financially; are you going to be financially secure? are you going to be rich beyond your wildest dreams? Tell 3 people today!

Day 10 — TALK ABOUT MONEY

Tasks for the day

1. TRACK ALL INCOME ON LOG

2. TELL 3 PEOPLE ACROSS THE DAY ABOUT YOUR WEALTH GOALS

3. LIST 3 THINGS THAT YOU'RE GRATEFUL FOR TODAY

4. REPEAT YOUR DAILY AFFIRMATION AT LEAST 3 TIMES

SHARE YOUR WINS ON SOCIAL MEDIA - TAG @CANNYCRYSTALS

@CANNYCRYSTALS   CANNYCRYSTALSACADEMY.CO.UK

Day 10 — TALK ABOUT MONEY

Gratitude

I am so grateful for....

because...

Affirmation of the day

"I AM GRATEFUL FOR ALL THE MONEY THAT PASSES THROUGH MY LIFE"

@CANNYCRYSTALS　　CANNYCRYSTALSACADEMY.CO.UK

Day 11 — REMIND YOURSELF

Reminding yourself of your goals daily plays a crucial role in the process of manifesting money. It serves as a powerful tool to keep your focus, motivation, and mindset aligned with your financial aspirations.

Setting financial goals is exciting, but maintaining motivation over the long term can be challenging. Daily goal reminders serve as constant reinforcement, keeping your objectives at the forefront of your mind. When you remind yourself of your goals every day, you tap into that initial enthusiasm and excitement, reigniting your motivation to take action and stay committed.

Personally, I like to set myself phone reminders to go off at points throughout the day with affirmations that remind me of the wealthy life I'm attempting to create for myself, such as "I'm wealthy beyond my wildest dreams" or "money shows up for me throughout the day unexpectedly".

Our beliefs about money and abundance shape our reality. By reminding yourself of your financial goals daily, you reinforce positive beliefs about your ability to achieve wealth and success. This repetition helps counteract any self-limiting beliefs or doubts that may arise along the way, replacing them with empowering thoughts and attitudes.

In our fast-paced and often distracting world, it's easy to lose sight of our goals. Daily goal reminders serve as a compass, keeping you focused and clear on your goals. They provide a constant reminder of the direction you want your financial life to take, helping you make decisions and prioritise actions that align with your goals.

Day 11 — REMIND YOURSELF

Visualisation is a powerful technique that you can use to remind yourself on a daily basis about your goals in manifesting money.

When you remind yourself of your goals daily, you reinforce the mental images and emotions associated with your financial desires. By consistently visualising the abundant life you want to create, you activate the creative power of your mind and align your subconscious with your conscious intentions.

Manifesting money requires consistent action and effort. Daily goal reminders serve as a call to action, prompting you to take small steps each day towards your financial objectives. They remind you that manifesting is not a passive process but an active and intentional pursuit that requires consistent effort and perseverance.

The path to financial abundance may have its ups and downs, and setbacks can test your determination. Daily goal reminders act as a source of strength and resilience during challenging times. They remind you of the bigger picture and help you stay focused on the long-term vision, enabling you to overcome obstacles and persist in the face of adversity.

To effectively remind yourself of your goals daily, consider incorporating practices such as visualisation, affirmations, journaling, or creating vision boards. These tools serve as tangible reminders that keep your goals present in your daily routine, allowing you to stay connected to your aspirations.

Today, we're going to set ourselves some reminders, either on our phone throughout the day, or by using sticky notes, and place them somewhere prominent, to remind us of the abundant, wealthy and prosperous beings that we are.

Day 11 — REMIND YOURSELF

Tasks for the day

1. TRACK ALL INCOME ON LOG

2. SET REMINDERS THROUGHOUT THE DAY ABOUT BEING WEALTHY

3. LIST 3 THINGS THAT YOU'RE GRATEFUL FOR TODAY

4. REPEAT YOUR DAILY AFFIRMATION AT LEAST 3 TIMES

SHARE YOUR WINS ON SOCIAL MEDIA - TAG @CANNYCRYSTALS

@CANNYCRYSTALS   CANNYCRYSTALSACADEMY.CO.UK

Day 11 — REMIND YOURSELF

Gratitude

I am so grateful for....

because...

Affirmation of the day

"I AM BLESSED TO RECEIVE MONEY IN LARGE AMOUNTS DAILY"

@CANNYCRYSTALS   CANNYCRYSTALSACADEMY.CO.UK

Day 12 — AN OPEN LETTER

Writing a letter to your future self is a powerful practice that can help you manifest more money and align your mindset with financial abundance.

Set aside dedicated time. Find a quiet and comfortable space where you can focus without distractions. Allocate enough time to reflect on your financial goals and aspirations and to write your letter thoughtfully.

Begin with a positive mindset. Approach the task with optimism and belief in your ability to manifest more money. Embrace an attitude of abundance and visualise yourself already achieving your desired financial success.

Start with a date: Begin the letter by addressing your future self with a specific date. For example, "Dear [Your Name], July 19, 2025."

Begin by expressing gratitude for the financial blessings you have already received and the progress you have made towards your goals. Acknowledge and appreciate any existing abundance in your life.

Write about the specific financial goals you want to manifest. Be specific, measurable, and realistic. Describe the lifestyle, experiences, or achievements that money will bring into your life. Visualise yourself already living and enjoying these financial achievements.

Use affirmations throughout the letter to reinforce your belief in your ability to manifest money. Affirm your worthiness, abundance, and capability to attract wealth. Repeat positive statements such as "I am deserving of financial abundance" or "Money flows to me effortlessly and abundantly."

Day 12 — AN OPEN LETTER

Write about the actions and steps you are taking or will take to manifest more money. This could include learning new skills, investing wisely, seeking opportunities, or enhancing your financial knowledge. Emphasise your commitment to taking consistent and inspired action towards your goals. Imagine your future self; close your eyes and visualise yourself in the future, living the abundant life you desire. Describe this vision in detail, incorporating all senses. Feel the joy, excitement, and fulfilment that comes with achieving your financial goals.

Conclude the letter with a positive and empowering note. Affirm your belief that you are on the right path, and express confidence in your ability to manifest money. Encourage your future self to continue pursuing financial abundance with determination and enthusiasm.

Then seal the letter; once you've completed the letter, fold it and seal it in an envelope. Consider writing an encouraging message on the outside of the envelope, such as "Open with joy and gratitude when you have manifested your financial dreams." Store the letter in a safe place. Keep the letter in a secure location, such as a personal journal, a special box, or even with a trusted friend or family member. Choose a place where you can access it at a later date, whether it's a few months or a few years from now.

Set a reminder in your calendar to open and read the letter on a specific future date. When that day arrives, take time to reflect on your financial journey and compare your current reality with the goals and aspirations you wrote about. Celebrate your progress and use the letter as a source of inspiration and motivation to continue manifesting financial abundance.

Day 12

AN OPEN LETTER

Tasks for the day

1. TRACK ALL INCOME ON LOG

2. WRITE YOURSELF AN ABUNDANCE LETTER

3. LIST 3 THINGS THAT YOU'RE GRATEFUL FOR TODAY

4. REPEAT YOUR DAILY AFFIRMATION AT LEAST 3 TIMES

SHARE YOUR WINS ON SOCIAL MEDIA - TAG @CANNYCRYSTALS

@CANNYCRYSTALS   CANNYCRYSTALSACADEMY.CO.UK

Day 12

AN OPEN LETTER

Gratitude

I am so grateful for....

because...

Affirmation of the day

"I AM A MAGNET FOR MONEY AND WEALTH IN ALL ITS FORMS"

@CANNYCRYSTALS CANNYCRYSTALSACADEMY.CO.UK

Day 13 — TREASURE HUNT

Finding money around your home can be a delightful surprise, and you might be surprised how much you can uncover with a little bit of exploration.

Here are some potential places to discover money around your home:

Couch Cushions and Upholstery: Check between the cushions of your couch or armchairs. Over time, loose change and even paper bills can find their way into these crevices.

Pockets: Before tossing your clothes in the washing machine, make sure to check the pockets. Money can often be forgotten and left in pockets of trousers, jackets, and even bags.

Jars and Containers: Many people have a habit of storing loose change in jars or containers. Check old piggy banks, mason jars, or even empty coffee cans.

Old Purses and Bags: If you have old purses, backpacks, or bags lying around, go through them. Coins or forgotten paper bills might be hiding in the pockets or folds.

Car: Search the seats, cup holders, and floor mats of your car. It's easy for change to accumulate over time.

Under Furniture: Occasionally, money can fall and get trapped under furniture like couches, beds, or dressers.

Old Electronics: If you have old phones, tablets, or gadgets, consider selling them. Websites and stores often offer money for used electronics.

Day 13   TREASURE HUNT

Old Toys: If you have children that no longer play with certain items, you could always sell these at a car boot sale.

Gift Cards: Occasionally, people give money as gifts in cards, and these might be overlooked or forgotten.

Treat your home like a treasure hunt. Start with one room and methodically work your way through each area. Focus on one spot at a time, thoroughly checking all potential hiding places in that area before moving on. This approach helps ensure you don't miss any spots.

If you live with family members or roommates, turn the search into a fun activity. Get everyone involved and assign different areas to each person. You can set a reward or share any findings as a small bonus for the participants.

As you search, take the opportunity to declutter and organise your belongings. Not only will this make the search more effective, but it can also help you find things you might have forgotten about, including money.

If you have storage areas like attics, basements, or old boxes, they can be treasure troves of forgotten items, including money. Carefully go through these spaces and look inside all containers and boxes.

In addition to cash, you might find valuable items or collectibles around your home that you can sell for money. Rare books, old coins, vintage items, or even valuable jewelry could be hidden in plain sight.

Finding money might take time, and you might not discover a significant amount all at once. Be patient - continue over time.

Day 13 — TREASURE HUNT

Tasks for the day

1. TRACK ALL INCOME ON LOG

2. GO ON A TREASURE HUNT AROUND YOUR HOME

3. LIST 3 THINGS THAT YOU'RE GRATEFUL FOR TODAY

4. REPEAT YOUR DAILY AFFIRMATION AT LEAST 3 TIMES

SHARE YOUR WINS ON SOCIAL MEDIA - TAG @CANNYCRYSTALS

@CANNYCRYSTALS CANNYCRYSTALSACADEMY.CO.UK

Day 13

TREASURE HUNT

Gratitude

I am so grateful for....

because...

Affirmation of the day

"I'M CAPABLE OF ACHIEVING ANY LEVEL OF FINANCIAL SUCCESS I DESIRE"

@CANNYCRYSTALS   CANNYCRYSTALSACADEMY.CO.UK

Day 14 — RELEASE IT

Releasing your attachment to wants and needs can be a powerful tool in manifesting wealth and financial abundance. When you release your strong attachment to specific outcomes or material possessions, you free yourself from the energy of lack and scarcity. This detachment allows you to approach manifesting wealth with a sense of ease and trust in the universe's abundance. By letting go of the "need" for money or specific outcomes, you open yourself up to receiving in unexpected and abundant ways.

Releasing wants and needs fosters gratitude for what you already have. Gratitude is a powerful vibration that aligns with abundance and attracts more positive experiences into your life. When you appreciate the abundance that already exists, you send a message to the universe that you are ready to receive even more blessings. By letting go of attachment to specific wants and needs, you shift your focus from scarcity to abundance consciousness. This mindset recognises the vast opportunities and resources available to you. It empowers you to approach manifesting wealth with confidence, knowing that you are supported by an abundant universe.

Releasing rigid expectations about how wealth should manifest in your life allows you to be more open and receptive to opportunities that may not have been on your radar. Sometimes the universe presents unexpected avenues for financial abundance, and by being open-minded, you can seize these opportunities and allow wealth to flow into your life.

Wanting and needing something too desperately can create resistance in the manifestation process. Resistance comes from a sense of lack or unworthiness, which hinders the flow of abundance.

Day 14 — RELEASE IT

Releasing wants and needs removes this resistance and allows you to be in a more receptive state, making it easier for wealth to come your way.

Releasing attachment to specific timelines for achieving wealth allows you to trust in divine timing. While it's essential to set goals and take action, trusting that everything will unfold at the right time allows you to stay patient and positive throughout the manifestation journey.

Remember that releasing wants and needs doesn't mean you shouldn't set clear intentions or take inspired actions towards your financial goals. It means approaching these goals with a sense of detachment, gratitude, and openness to receive wealth in various forms.

Trust that the universe is abundant and ready to support you in your journey towards financial prosperity.

Today, we're going to write a list of all the things in our life that we want to release and let go. Once we have our list, I'd like you to give thanks to each individual thing, for however it's served you, and I'd like you to truly feel those feelings building up inside of you.

When the time feels right, we're then going to set alight to our list. Please ensure that when you do this, that you're doing so in a safe environment such as a metal kitchen sink basin, or a fire-proof dish in a suitable outdoor space.

If you don't want to set alight to your list, you can always rip it up, bury it, or dispose of it however you choose to do so. As you do this, imagine everything releasing from your body, ready to make room for abundance to flow in.

Day 14 — RELEASE IT

Tasks for the day

1. TRACK ALL INCOME ON LOG

2. WRITE A RELEASE LIST, FEEL THOSE EMOTIONS, AND BURN IT

3. LIST 3 THINGS THAT YOU'RE GRATEFUL FOR TODAY

4. REPEAT YOUR DAILY AFFIRMATION AT LEAST 3 TIMES

SHARE YOUR WINS ON SOCIAL MEDIA - TAG @CANNYCRYSTALS

@CANNYCRYSTALS   CANNYCRYSTALSACADEMY.CO.UK

Day 14

RELEASE IT

Gratitude

I am so grateful for....

because...

Affirmation of the day

"I AM A MAGNET FOR WEALTH, AND IT FINDS ME WHEREVER I GO"

@CANNYCRYSTALS CANNYCRYSTALSACADEMY.CO.UK

Day 15 — GRATITUDE

Gratitude is of paramount importance in manifesting and attracting money into your life. When you cultivate a mindset of gratitude, it positively influences your thoughts, emotions, and actions, all of which play a crucial role in the manifestation process.

Gratitude helps shift your focus from a mindset of scarcity and lack to one of abundance. When you are grateful for what you already have, you attract more positive experiences and resources into your life. Instead of dwelling on what you don't have, gratitude helps you appreciate the wealth and abundance that already exists in your life. Gratitude is a high-vibrational emotion. When you feel grateful, you emit positive energy into the universe. The law of attraction states that like attracts like, so when you vibrate at a higher frequency, you're more likely to attract positive circumstances, including financial opportunities.

A positive mindset is essential for manifesting and attracting money. Gratitude nurtures a positive outlook, which allows you to see opportunities and solutions rather than dwelling on problems or obstacles. A positive mindset makes you more open to wealth-generating possibilities. Gratitude creates a sense of openness and receptivity. When you're grateful, you acknowledge and accept the gifts and blessings that come your way, including financial abundance. Being open to receiving is vital for allowing money to flow into your life.

Gratitude has a positive impact on your emotional well-being. It reduces stress and anxiety, which can cloud your judgment and hinder your ability to make clear financial decisions. When you are less stressed, you can think more rationally and make better financial choices.

Day 15 — GRATITUDE

Expressing gratitude fosters strong and supportive relationships with others. Grateful individuals are more likely to build positive connections and networks, which can lead to new opportunities and collaborations that may contribute to financial success.

Gratitude encourages responsible financial behaviour. When you are grateful for the money you have, you are more likely to manage it wisely and avoid overspending. This financial responsibility can lead to increased savings and investments, contributing to your financial well-being. It also nurtures self-worth and self-confidence. When you acknowledge your abilities and accomplishments, you develop a stronger sense of self-belief. This self-belief can empower you to pursue opportunities and take risks that may lead to financial prosperity.

Gratitude also helps you recognise that you are already abundant in many ways. By focusing on the abundance you have, you attract more abundance into your life. This sense of abundance encourages a positive outlook and increases the likelihood of financial opportunities. Gratitude can be a motivating factor. When you are grateful for the financial opportunities that come your way, you are more likely to take action and seize those opportunities. Taking action is essential for manifesting money and turning your goals into reality. It shifts your mindset, emotions, and actions, making you more open, positive, and receptive to financial abundance. By cultivating gratitude, you align yourself with the energy of wealth and abundance, which can lead to attracting more money and prosperity into your life.

Today, write a list of 10 reasons why you're grateful for money. If you struggle with this, think how life would be without it.

Day 15 — GRATITUDE

Tasks for the day

1. TRACK ALL INCOME ON LOG

2. WRITE A LIST OF 10 REASONS TO BE GRATEFUL FOR MONEY

3. LIST 3 THINGS THAT YOU'RE GRATEFUL FOR TODAY

4. REPEAT YOUR DAILY AFFIRMATION AT LEAST 3 TIMES

SHARE YOUR WINS ON SOCIAL MEDIA - TAG @CANNYCRYSTALS

@CANNYCRYSTALS CANNYCRYSTALSACADEMY.CO.UK

Day 15 — GRATITUDE

Gratitude

I am so grateful for....

because...

Affirmation of the day

"I AM WORTHY OF RECEIVING UNLIMITED FINANCIAL BLESSINGS"

@CANNYCRYSTALS   CANNYCRYSTALSACADEMY.CO.UK

Day 16 — ALIGN YOUR ACTIONS

Aligning our actions in life is essential for successful manifestation because our actions are the physical expression of our thoughts, beliefs, and intentions. When our actions are in harmony with our desires and goals, we create a powerful synergy that accelerates the manifestation process.

When we align our actions with our intentions, we gain clarity about what we truly want to manifest. This alignment helps us focus our energy and attention on specific goals, making it easier for the universe to understand and respond to our intentions.

Aligning our actions requires consistent effort and commitment. When we are dedicated to taking action towards our desires, we demonstrate our sincerity and determination to manifest them, which reinforces the strength of our intentions.

Taking aligned actions generates positive energy and high vibrations. Positive actions are in harmony with our desires, and this energy attracts more positive circumstances and opportunities that align with what we want to manifest.

Sometimes, we may have subconscious blocks or limiting beliefs that hinder our manifestation. By aligning our actions, we confront and overcome these resistance points, allowing us to move forward with greater ease.

When we act in alignment with our goals, it reinforces our beliefs in the possibility of achieving them. Aligning our actions can also be a form of visualisation, as we engage in activities that mirror the reality we want to manifest.

Day 16 — ALIGN YOUR ACTIONS

Taking aligned actions creates momentum towards our goals. Each step forward builds upon the previous one, propelling us closer to our desired outcomes.

As we align our actions, we become more attuned to recognising and seizing opportunities that lead us towards our manifestation goals. Aligned actions can inspire and influence others in a positive way. This can attract like-minded individuals or collaborators who support our desires and goals, enhancing the manifestation process.

Taking action aligned with our desires instils a sense of empowerment and self-belief. This self-assurance reinforces our manifestation efforts and attracts even more positive outcomes.

The universe responds to the signals we send through our actions. When our actions are aligned with our intentions, we create a harmonious resonance that attracts the desired manifestations into our lives.

In summary, aligning our actions with our intentions is a critical aspect of successful manifestation. It involves clarity, commitment, positive energy, and consistent effort towards our goals.

By taking action in harmony with our desires, we create a powerful force that attracts the people, circumstances, and opportunities needed to manifest our dreams into reality.

Today, have a think about how you can align your actions with your full intentions around raising your wealth and abundance. Ask yourself, are there any actions that are going against what you're trying to achieve?

Day 16 — ALIGN YOUR ACTIONS

Tasks for the day

1. TRACK ALL INCOME ON LOG

2. THINK ABOUT HOW YOU CAN ALIGN YOUR DAILY ACTIONS

3. LIST 3 THINGS THAT YOU'RE GRATEFUL FOR TODAY

4. REPEAT YOUR DAILY AFFIRMATION AT LEAST 3 TIMES

SHARE YOUR WINS ON SOCIAL MEDIA - TAG @CANNYCRYSTALS

@CANNYCRYSTALS   CANNYCRYSTALSACADEMY.CO.UK

Day 16 — ALIGN YOUR ACTIONS

Gratitude

I am so grateful for....

because...

Affirmation of the day

"MONEY COMES TO ME EASILY AND EFFORTLESSLY"

@CANNYCRYSTALS CANNYCRYSTALSACADEMY.CO.UK

Day 17 — MINDFULNESS

Mindfulness can be a powerful tool to attract wealth into your life by helping you become more aware of your thoughts, emotions, and actions related to money.

Practice mindfulness to become aware of any limiting beliefs or negative associations you have with money. Notice the thoughts and emotions that arise when you think about wealth. By identifying and acknowledging these beliefs, you can work on replacing them with positive and empowering ones.

You can use mindfulness to shift your focus from scarcity to abundance. Pay attention to the blessings and abundance already present in your life. Cultivate gratitude for the money you have and the opportunities available to you. This positive mindset attracts more wealth and prosperity.

When you engage in mindful visualisation of your financial goals. Imagine yourself achieving success and experiencing abundance. Visualisation creates a powerful subconscious alignment with your desires and helps attract opportunities to manifest your dreams.

Be mindful of your financial decisions. Pause before making purchases or investments, and consider whether they align with your goals. Avoid impulsive spending and make conscious choices to use your money wisely.

Mindfulness can help you manage financial stress and anxiety. When you feel overwhelmed, take a moment to practice deep breathing or meditation to calm your mind. Reducing stress allows you to think more clearly and make better financial decisions.

Day 17 — MINDFULNESS

Express gratitude for the money that comes into your life. Whether it's through your job, investments, or unexpected windfalls, being grateful for money opens you up to receiving more of it.

Mindfulness teaches us to let go of attachment to outcomes. While it's essential to set financial goals, being overly attached to specific results can create stress and resistance. Trust in the process, take inspired actions and release attachment to the how and when of achieving wealth.

Mindfulness helps you stay present and attentive to your surroundings. This heightened awareness enables you to recognise financial opportunities that you might have otherwise overlooked. Mindfulness teaches us to stay focused on our own path without comparing ourselves to others. Comparing your financial situation to others can lead to feelings of lack and hinder your wealth manifestation.

Be mindful of the power of giving. Contribute to others and charitable causes without expecting anything in return. Giving freely creates a sense of abundance and attracts positive energy.

By integrating mindfulness practices into your daily routine, you can enhance your ability to attract wealth and create a more abundant and prosperous future.

Today, try to ground yourself in the present moment, either through some form of meditation or mindful practice. We can manifest money with mindfulness by cultivating a positive and grateful mindset, staying present in financial decisions, and recognising and seizing opportunities aligned with our desires.

Day 17 — MINDFULNESS

Tasks for the day

1. TRACK ALL INCOME ON LOG

2. TRY TO BE MINDFUL THROUGHOUT THE DAY

3. LIST 3 THINGS THAT YOU'RE GRATEFUL FOR TODAY

4. REPEAT YOUR DAILY AFFIRMATION AT LEAST 3 TIMES

SHARE YOUR WINS ON SOCIAL MEDIA - TAG @CANNYCRYSTALS

@CANNYCRYSTALS CANNYCRYSTALSACADEMY.CO.UK

Day 17

MINDFULNESS

Gratitude

I am so grateful for....

because...

Affirmation of the day

"I AM FINANCIALLY FREE AND ABUNDANT"

@CANNYCRYSTALS CANNYCRYSTALSACADEMY.CO.UK

Day 18 GIVING AND DONATING

Giving and donating can significantly enhance your money mindset in several ways; it helps to shift your focus from scarcity to abundance. When you act from a place of generosity, you reinforce the belief that there is enough to share, fostering an abundance mindset that attracts more wealth.

Giving to others cultivates gratitude for the resources and wealth you already possess, reinforcing a positive outlook on your financial situation.

Being generous builds empathy and strengthens your connection with others. This positive social connection can lead to new opportunities and collaborations that may contribute to your financial growth. By giving and donating, you shift your focus from self-centeredness to the well-being of others. This perspective can help reduce financial stress and improve your overall money mindset.

Contributing to causes you care about can bring a sense of fulfilment and purpose to your life, enhancing your overall well-being and financial satisfaction.

Giving demonstrates your belief in an abundant universe where there is enough for everyone. This belief can attract more opportunities and financial abundance into your life.

Donating money also allows you to contribute to positive change and make a difference in the world, increasing your sense of empowerment and financial self-worth.

By giving and donating, you practice detachment from money, acknowledging that it is a tool to create positive impact and experiences rather than a source of identity or validation.

Day 18 GIVING AND DONATING

Acts of giving can boost your self-esteem and self-worth, making you feel more deserving of financial abundance and success.

Giving and donating generate positive energy and good karma. This positive energy can attract more positive financial opportunities into your life. Giving and donating can profoundly impact your money mindset by reinforcing abundance, gratitude, and empathy. As you contribute to others, you create a positive cycle of prosperity and attract more financial opportunities and wealth into your life.

Now, obviously, when I talk about giving and donating, this doesn't necessarily mean that you have to give up your hard earned money to receive more in return. If you feel you want to donate to a cause generously, by all means do that, but don't feel that you have to use your last bit of money to give to some cause.

When decluttering your home on Day 5 for example, you could have donated all that you no longer wanted to a homeless shelter, or a charity close to your heart.

You can also give your time - it doesn't have to be something physical. Giving your time to someone by helping out or volunteering can be really helpful to them, but can also help to raise your own self esteem and confidence too.

Today, think about how you can either donate or give. The universe knows that when we give out, we're in the mindset of there being more than enough in the world, and we live with an abundant mindset, which it then rewards with more situations to feel abundant about.

Day 18 — GIVING AND DONATING

Tasks for the day

1. TRACK ALL INCOME ON LOG

2. GIVE OR DONATE SOMETHING TODAY (TIME, OBJECTS, ETC.)

3. LIST 3 THINGS THAT YOU'RE GRATEFUL FOR TODAY

4. REPEAT YOUR DAILY AFFIRMATION AT LEAST 3 TIMES

SHARE YOUR WINS ON SOCIAL MEDIA - TAG @CANNYCRYSTALS

@CANNYCRYSTALS   CANNYCRYSTALSACADEMY.CO.UK

Day 18 — GIVING AND DONATING

Gratitude

I am so grateful for....

because...

Affirmation of the day

"I AM A WISE STEWARD OF MY FINANCES"

@CANNYCRYSTALS   CANNYCRYSTALSACADEMY.CO.UK

Day 19   SELF-REFLECTION

Self-reflection plays a crucial role in attracting money into your life by providing insights into your thoughts, beliefs, behaviours, and mindset related to finances.

Through self-reflection, you can become aware of any limiting beliefs you have about money, such as "I don't deserve wealth" or "Money is the root of all evil." Recognising these beliefs allows you to work on replacing them with more empowering and positive ones that align with your financial goals.

Self-reflection helps you understand your financial habits and patterns. You can identify any unproductive spending behaviours or areas where you could improve your money management skills. Reflecting on your financial goals helps you gain clarity about what you truly want to achieve. By understanding your aspirations, you can create a more focused and purposeful plan for attracting money.

Self-reflection also allows you to explore your relationship with money. This includes how you view money, whether you see it as a positive tool for growth or a source of stress and anxiety. Understanding your relationship with money helps you shift towards a healthier and more positive mindset.

Celebrate your financial achievements through self-reflection. Acknowledging past successes, no matter how small reinforces a positive money mindset and boosts your confidence in attracting more abundance.

Self-reflection helps you learn from financial mistakes or setbacks. Instead of dwelling on failures, you can extract valuable lessons that can lead to better financial decisions in the future.

Day 19 — SELF-REFLECTION

Self-reflection allows you to practice gratitude for the money you have and the financial opportunities available to you. Gratitude is a powerful tool for attracting more abundance into your life. By reflecting on your financial thoughts and behaviours, you increase self-awareness. This awareness helps you catch any negative thought patterns or self-sabotaging behaviours that might hinder your money manifestation efforts.

Through self-reflection, you can set realistic and achievable financial intentions. Understanding your current financial situation and capabilities enables you to create goals that align with your current circumstances. Self-reflection guides you in taking actions that align with your financial aspirations. It helps you make conscious decisions and stay committed to your money goals. By becoming aware of your beliefs, habits, and intentions related to money, you can make positive changes that align with your financial goals and pave the way for greater abundance and prosperity.

One task you can do today is to journal about your money beliefs and attitudes. Take some time to sit down with a notebook or a digital journal and answer the following prompts:

1. Beliefs about Money: Write down your beliefs about money. Are they mostly positive and empowering, or do you notice any limiting beliefs?
2. Past Money Experiences: Reflect on your past experiences with money, both positive and negative. How have these experiences shaped your current money mindset?
3. Current Financial Situation: Assess your current financial situation. How do you feel about it? Are you satisfied with where you are financially, or do you feel a sense of lack or stress?

Day 19 — SELF-REFLECTION

Tasks for the day

1. TRACK ALL INCOME ON LOG

2. SELF-REFLECT THROUGH THE JOURNAL PROMPTS PROVIDED

3. LIST 3 THINGS THAT YOU'RE GRATEFUL FOR TODAY

4. REPEAT YOUR DAILY AFFIRMATION AT LEAST 3 TIMES

SHARE YOUR WINS ON SOCIAL MEDIA - TAG @CANNYCRYSTALS

@CANNYCRYSTALS   CANNYCRYSTALSACADEMY.CO.UK

Day 19 — SELF-REFLECTION

Gratitude

I am so grateful for....

because...

Affirmation of the day

"I AM SURROUNDED BY AN ABUNDANCE OF OPPORTUNITIES"

@CANNYCRYSTALS CANNYCRYSTALSACADEMY.CO.UK

Day 20   SELF-DEVELOPMENT

Self-development is of paramount importance in your money mindset journey as it lays the foundation for attracting financial abundance and creating a prosperous life. It brings awareness to your limiting beliefs about money that may be holding you back. Through personal growth, you can identify and challenge these beliefs, replacing them with more empowering ones that support your financial goals.

Self-development also fosters a growth mindset, which is essential for embracing challenges and seeing them as opportunities for learning and improvement. With a growth mindset, setbacks are viewed as temporary, and you are more likely to persist in your money manifestation journey.

As you invest in self-development, you build confidence in your abilities and increase your self-worth. This newfound belief in yourself can empower you to take bolder actions and pursue opportunities that lead to financial growth.

Self-development often involves acquiring new skills, including financial literacy and money management. By enhancing your financial knowledge, you can make informed decisions and effectively manage your money. It also improves emotional intelligence, allowing you to understand and manage your emotions better, especially when it comes to money-related decisions. Emotional intelligence helps you make rational choices and avoid impulsive financial behaviours.

Self-development helps you clarify your values and set specific and achievable financial goals aligned with your aspirations. With clear goals, you can create actionable plans to work towards manifesting wealth.

Day 20 — SELF-DEVELOPMENT

Through self-development, you cultivate a positive money mindset that attracts abundance and prosperity. Positive thinking and a belief in the abundance of the universe contribute to your ability to manifest money.

Self-development provides tools and techniques to face and overcome financial fears. Whether it's fear of failure or fear of success, working on yourself allows you to confront and conquer these fears.

It also often involves networking and building meaningful connections with others. These connections can lead to collaborations and partnerships that open up new financial opportunities.

Self-development encourages a holistic approach to wealth, encompassing not only financial well-being but also emotional, mental, and physical well-being. When you prioritise overall well-being, it positively impacts your financial journey.

As you grow and develop, you naturally become more responsible with your finances. You become mindful of spending habits, prioritize saving and investing, and manage money with prudence. It empowers you to break free from limiting beliefs, cultivate positive habits, and take proactive steps toward financial abundance. By investing in yourself and your personal growth, you create a strong foundation for attracting wealth and achieving your financial goals with confidence and purpose.

Today, take some time to look into a self-development course, or read a book, or watch a programme - something that will feed your brain and develop you around your money mindset.

Day 20 — SELF-DEVELOPMENT

Tasks for the day

1. TRACK ALL INCOME ON LOG

2. DEVELOP YOURSELF THROUGH A BOOK, COURSE OR SHOW

3. LIST 3 THINGS THAT YOU'RE GRATEFUL FOR TODAY

4. REPEAT YOUR DAILY AFFIRMATION AT LEAST 3 TIMES

SHARE YOUR WINS ON SOCIAL MEDIA - TAG @CANNYCRYSTALS

@CANNYCRYSTALS   CANNYCRYSTALSACADEMY.CO.UK

Day 20 — SELF-DEVELOPMENT

Gratitude

I am so grateful for....

because...

Affirmation of the day

"I AM ABUNDANT IN EVERY AREA OF MY LIFE"

@CANNYCRYSTALS CANNYCRYSTALSACADEMY.CO.UK

Day 21 — WRAPPING UP

By taking all of the last 20 days into account, you're now well prepped to start changing your mindset around money, which will help you to attract more of it into your life.

Start with Gratitude: Begin each day with a gratitude practice. Take a few moments to express thanks for the money you have, the opportunities available to you, and the abundance in your life.

Self-Reflection and Journaling: Dedicate time for self-reflection and journaling regularly. Write about your money beliefs, past experiences, current financial situation, and your financial goals. Use journaling to challenge limiting beliefs and reinforce positive affirmations.

Set Clear Financial Goals: Define specific and achievable financial goals. Be clear about what you want to manifest and create a plan to reach those goals.

Practice Mindfulness: Incorporate mindfulness into your daily routine. Practice deep breathing, meditation, or mindfulness exercises to reduce stress, increase self-awareness, and make conscious financial decisions.

Embrace a Growth Mindset: Adopt a growth mindset that views challenges as opportunities for growth. Cultivate resilience and determination in pursuing your financial goals.

Manage Emotions: Be aware of your emotions around money. Practice emotional intelligence to make rational decisions and avoid impulsive spending or investing based on emotions.

Day 21 — WRAPPING UP

Practice Giving and Sharing: Contribute to others and charitable causes regularly. Give without expecting anything in return, knowing that your act of giving fosters a sense of abundance and attracts positive energy.

Build Positive Connections: Network and build positive relationships with like-minded individuals. Surround yourself with people who support your financial aspirations and encourage your growth.

Visualise and Affirm: Engage in regular visualization of your financial success. Use positive affirmations related to wealth and abundance to reinforce your beliefs in attracting money.

Stay Aligned with Your Goals: Continuously align your actions with your financial goals. Take consistent steps towards manifesting wealth, and be open to recognising and seizing opportunities that align with your desires.

Practice Self-Compassion: Be kind to yourself on your money mindset journey. Understand that change takes time, and it's okay to make mistakes. Treat yourself with self-compassion as you grow and evolve. Be patient with yourself and stay committed to your personal growth and financial goals. By incorporating these elements into your life consistently, you create a powerful synergy that supports your manifestation of wealth and abundance.

To go further with this, don't forget, I also have a 6 week manifesting money masterclass available at my website, which you can get lifetime access at 50% off by using code MONEYMONEYMONEY

Abundance, wealth and prosperity to you on your money mindset journey.

Day 21

WRAPPING UP

Tasks for the day

1. TRACK ALL INCOME ON LOG

2. REFLECT ON THE LAST 3 WEEKS WORTH OF THIS CHALLENGE

3. LIST 3 THINGS THAT YOU'RE GRATEFUL FOR TODAY

4. REPEAT YOUR DAILY AFFIRMATION AT LEAST 3 TIMES

SHARE YOUR WINS ON SOCIAL MEDIA - TAG @CANNYCRYSTALS

@CANNYCRYSTALS   CANNYCRYSTALSACADEMY.CO.UK

Day 21 — WRAPPING UP

Gratitude

I am so grateful for....

because...

Affirmation of the day

"I AM FILLED WITH PROSPERITY AND WEALTH"

@CANNYCRYSTALS CANNYCRYSTALSACADEMY.CO.UK

Thank you

THANK YOU FOR TAKING PART IN THIS
21 DAY CHALLENGE!

I really hope that you've enjoyed it. Don't forget to check out all of the other courses and masterclasses as cannycrystalsacademy.co.uk

Follow me on Instagram, TikTok and Facebook:

@cannycrystals
@marttweedy

If you have any further queries, please don't hesitate to drop us an email at info@cannycrystals.co.uk

All the very best for your manifesting money journey!

Mart

@CANNYCRYSTALS   CANNYCRYSTALSACADEMY.CO.UK

Notes

Notes

Notes

Notes

Notes

@CANNYCRYSTALS   CANNYCRYSTALSACADEMY.CO.UK

Notes

@CANNYCRYSTALS   CANNYCRYSTALSACADEMY.CO.UK

Printed in Poland
by Amazon Fulfillment
Poland Sp. z o.o., Wrocław